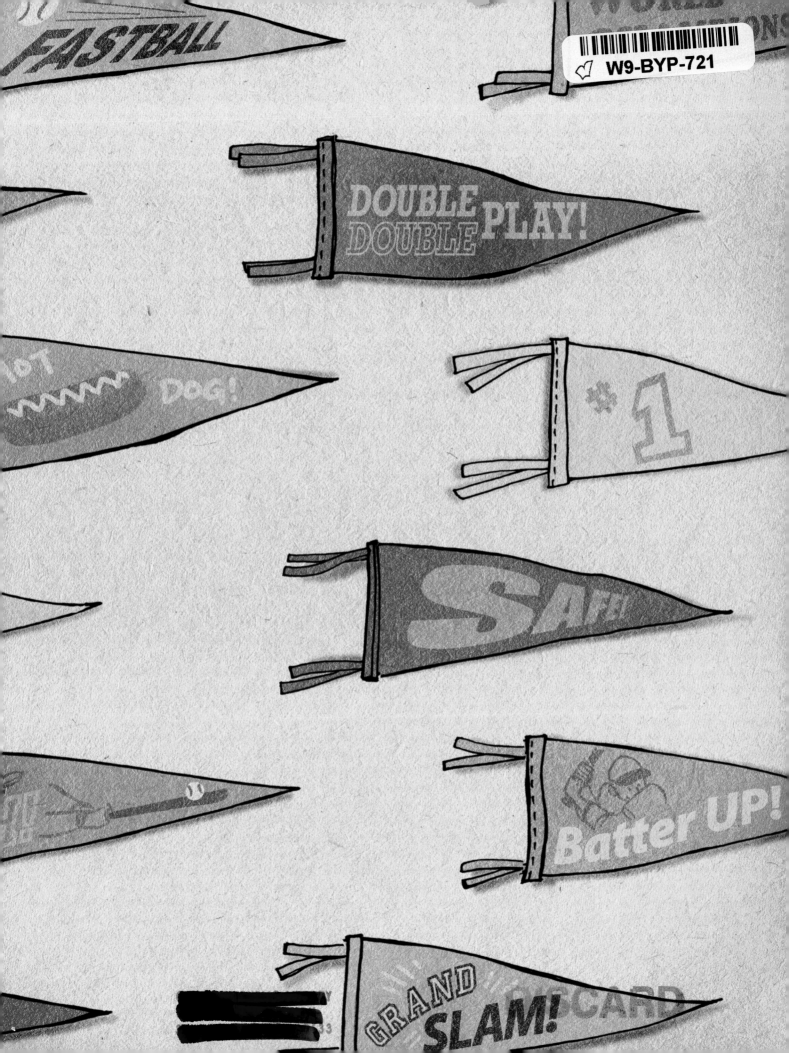

Chronicle Books would like to extend a special thanks
to John Horne of the National Baseball Hall of Fame for all
his help in gathering the historical photographs compiled in this book.

Book design by Sara Gillingham.
Text by Lisa McGuinness.

IMAGE CREDITS:
Illustrations © 2009 by David Habben: pages 16, 19, 20, 22, 25, 28, 32, 34–35, 36–37, and endpapers
Photographs/Artwork © istockphoto.com: ball, page 5; bat, page 5; glove, page 13;
child player, page 19; metal bat, page 20; softball, page 27
All other photographs are © National Baseball Hall of Fame Library, Cooperstown, New York

Typeset in Fenway Park, Forward Passed, and Futura.
Manufactured in China.

Library of Congress Cataloging-in-Publication Data
B is for baseball : running the bases from A to Z.
p. cm.
ISBN 978-0-8118-6096-3
1. Baseball—Juvenile literature. 2. Alphabet books. I. Title.
GV867.5.D2 2009
796.357—dc22
2008026512

10 9 8 7 6 5 4 3 2 1

Chronicle Books LLC
680 Second Street, San Francisco, California 94107

www.chroniclekids.com

B Is for BASEBALL

RUNNING THE BASES FROM A TO Z

chronicle books · san francisco

AUTOGRAPH
the signature of a
baseball player

MILWAUKEE, 1944

ALL-AMERICAN GIRLS PROFESSIONAL BASEBALL LEAGUE

a special league for women that lasted from 1943 to 1954

Babe Ruth

He said, "Never let the fear of striking out get in your way."

1921

WILLIE MAYS

BATTER

the player who swings the bat at the ball to try to get a hit

BALL

made of cork, rubber, and yarn, then covered in two pieces of white leather and fastened with 216 stitches (108 double stitches)

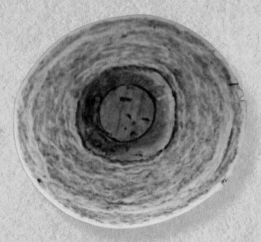

YOGI BERRA, CIRCA 1956

C

CATCHER
plays behind home plate and catches
the balls that are thrown by the pitcher

CENTER FIELD
the middle part of the outfield

CAP
keeps the sun out of players' eyes when they are out in the field

DUGOUT
where the players keep their
equipment and stay during the game

CLEVELAND INDIANS, 1941

DODGERS
played in Brooklyn from 1890 to 1957
and then moved to Los Angeles in 1958

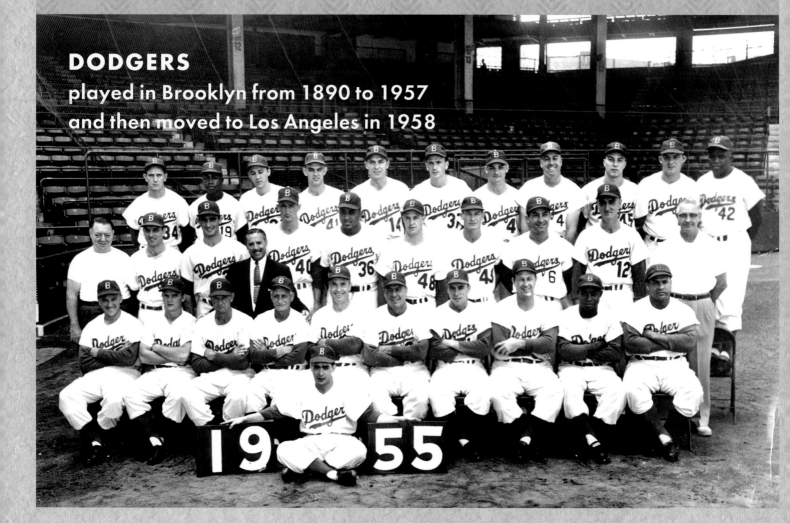

19 55

EXCITEMENT
the way people feel when lots of action happens in the game

FANS AT EBBETS FIELD, 1955

ERROR
when a player makes a mistake
when fielding the ball

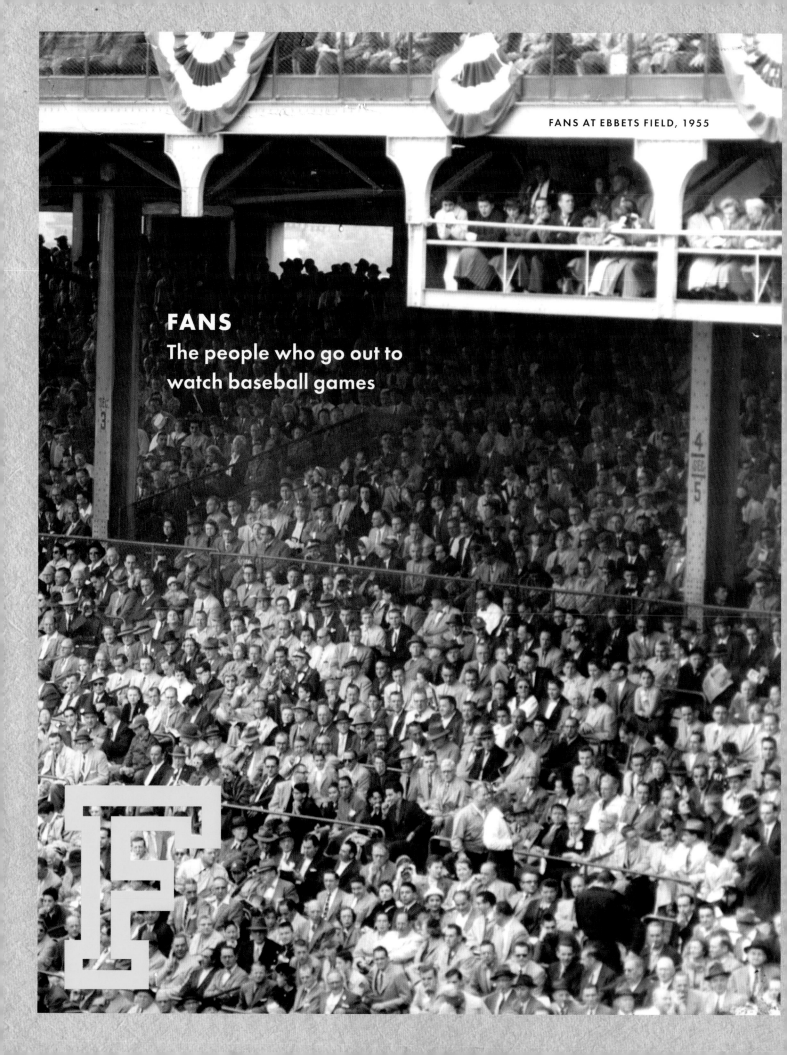

FANS AT EBBETS FIELD, 1955

FANS
The people who go out to watch baseball games

GLOVE
padded hand-covering a player uses to catch the ball

FENWAY PARK

GRASS
covers baseball fields except along the bases and the pitcher's mound

H

HELMET
protects a batter's head
while up at bat

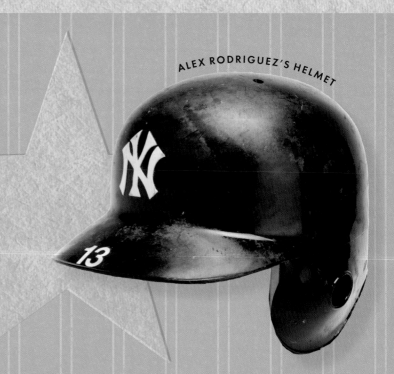

ALEX RODRIGUEZ'S HELMET

YANKEE STADIUM, 1947

HOT DOGS
one of the favorite snacks found at baseball parks

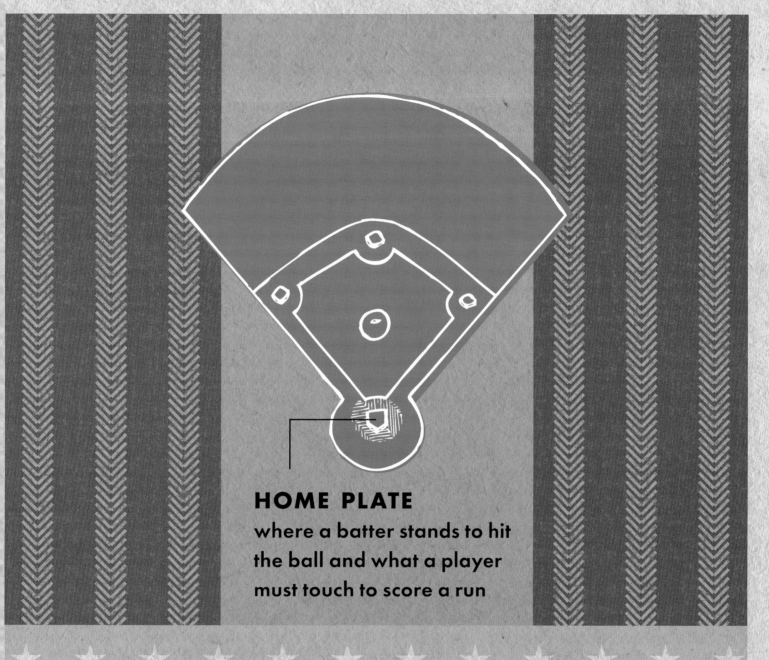

HOME PLATE
where a batter stands to hit the ball and what a player must touch to score a run

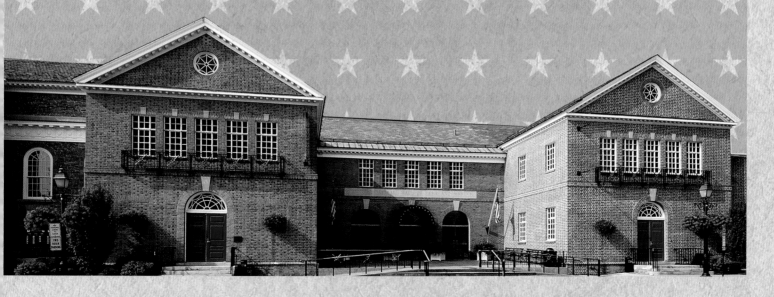

HALL OF FAME
a world-famous baseball museum in Cooperstown, New York

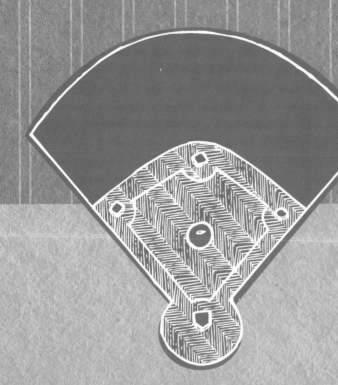

INFIELD
the part of the baseball field from the bases to home plate

INFIELDERS
players who field close-hit balls and try to get the runners out at the bases

TINKERS, EVERS, AND CHANCE (1910) WERE KNOWN AS
THE BEST INFIELD COMBINATION IN HISTORY

J

Joe DiMaggio

Known as one of the best players in baseball history, he got hits in 56 consecutive games.

Jackie Robinson

the first African American baseball player to play in the Major Leagues

K

Abbreviation for a strikeout. A backward K means the player struck out without swinging the bat.

MOOKIE WILSON AT BAT, 1986

KNUCKLEBALL

when a pitcher uses his knuckles to throw the ball

PHIL NIEKRO, HIGH SCHOOL PHOTO, CIRCA 1956

Little League

a baseball league for children

LEFT FIELD
part of the outfield, between third and second bases

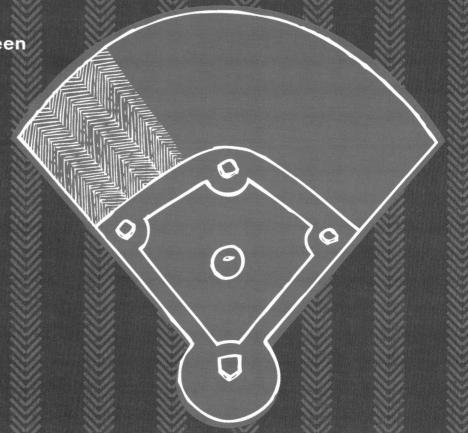

Major League

the highest level of professional baseball

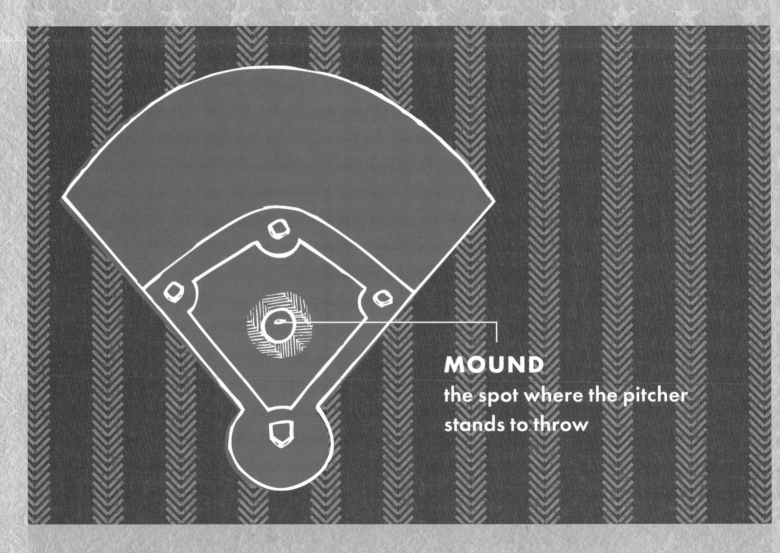

MOUND
the spot where the pitcher
stands to throw

METAL BAT

first on the scene in 1924, but still not
allowed in the Major League, where
bats have to be made of wood

NATIONAL ANTHEM
sung before the start of all Major League baseball games

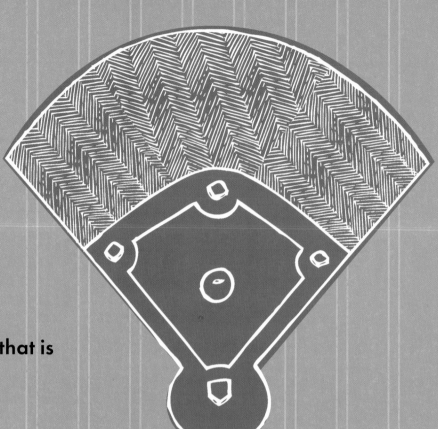

OUTFIELD
the part of the field that is past the bases

OUT!
If a batter's hit ball is caught before it bounces or a fielder gets the ball to the base before the runner, that player is out.

BERNIE CARBO OF THE REDS GETS CALLED OUT AT HOME PLATE IN THE 1970 WORLD SERIES

PEANUTS
nuts that are sold by the bag at baseball parks

PITCHER
the player who throws the balls across home plate that the batter tries to hit

TOM SEAVER

GARY CARTER, 1986

Q&A (Questions & Answers)
Oftentimes after important games, baseball players are interviewed by the press.

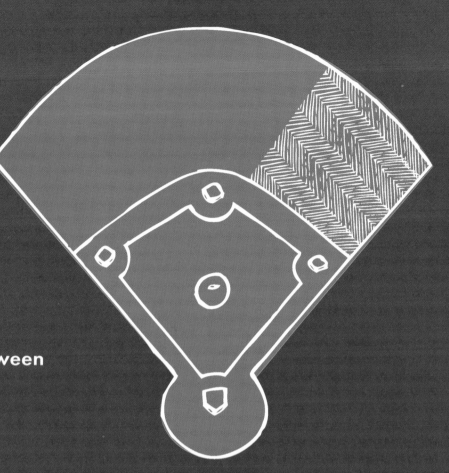

RIGHT FIELD
part of the outfield, between first and second bases

ROSTER
the list of players on a team

New York Yankees 1927 World Champions Team Roster

Julie Wera	Mark Koenig	Lou Gehrig	Don Miller
Mike Gazella	Bob Shawkey	Herb Pennock	Bob Meusel
Urban Shocker	Dutch Ruether	Tony Lazzeri	Waite Hoyt
Joe Dugan	Johnny Grabowski	Wilcy Moore	Joe Giard
Earle Combs	George Pipgras	Babe Ruth	

SAFE!

When a runner reaches the base before the fielders get the ball to the base, the player is safe.

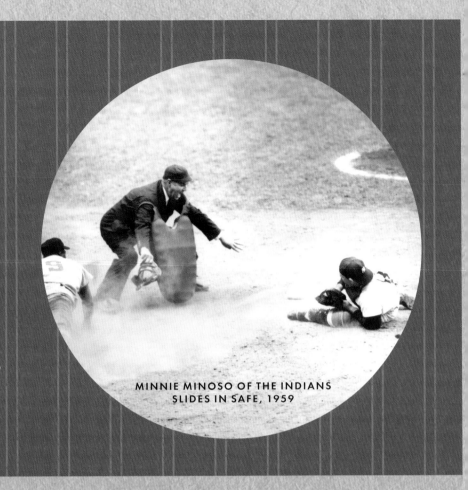

MINNIE MINOSO OF THE INDIANS
SLIDES IN SAFE, 1959

SLIDE

When runners are trying to reach a base before the ball they sometimes slide into the base.

WILLIE MAYS 1954

STADIUM
the large building that surrounds a baseball field, with lots of stands for fans to sit and watch the game

CAMDEN YARDS

SOFTBALL
a ball that is softer and larger than a baseball and is pitched underhand

TEAM
one group of players who are playing against another group of players

NEW YORK YANKEES, 1927

THROW
when players toss the ball

TAG
Another way to get an "out" is to tag a runner before he or she touches the base.

U

UNIFORM
special clothes players
wear to show that they
are on the same team

UMPIRE
who makes sure the rules are
followed and decides when
pitches are strikes or balls
and whether players are "safe"
or "out"

1941

VISITORS
the team that comes from another place to play baseball against the "home team"

VICTORY
The winners celebrate their victory.

METS CELEBRATE THEIR GAME 6 VICTORY
OF THE 1986 WORLD SERIES

WOMEN'S LEAGUE
baseball teams made up
of only women

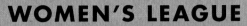

Willie Mays

One of the best center fielders of
all time, he hit 660 home runs in his
Major League baseball career.

1950s

PLAYER	1	2	3	4	5	6	7	8	9	10	11
SS McGuinness, Natasha	SB BB		K		L4			1-3	SB PC		
2B Davis, Dan	CS 1B		P7			L5		BB	K		
1B McFerrin, Cashey	K			K			P9	HR			P8
CF McGuinness, Matt		BB			K		2B		P9		K
RF Rundle, Ben		K			E4 1B		5-3		SB 1B		SB 1B
LF Stephenson, Jack			6-3		P-7			K K	1-3		
3B McFerrin, Riley				K		2B		2B	2B	BB	6-3
C Stephenson, Audrey				6-3	K	K	K	K	1B		K
P McGuinness, Jordan	1 / 1	0 / 0	0 / 0	0 / 0	0 / 0	0 / 1	1 / 1	1 / 2	2 / 1	0 / 0	0

X-TRA INNINGS

When a game is tied after
nine innings, it continues
into "extra innings."

野球

YAKYU
the name for "baseball" in Japanese

Yogi Berra

known as one of the best catchers of all time

ZONE

the area that a pitch must be thrown
into to be considered a "strike"

ZINGER

a nickname for a "grounder"

Z

LEFT FIELD

3RD BASE

DUGOUT

PITCHER'S MOUND

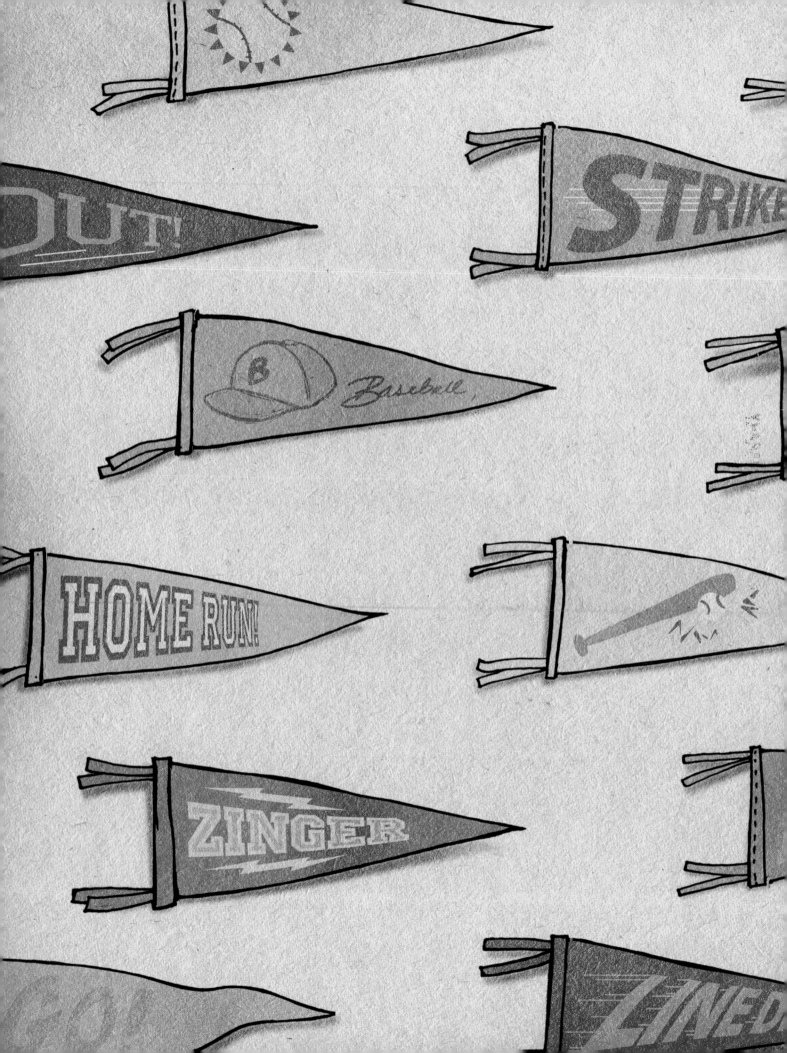